S0-BDM-172

IMAGES
of America

GIRL SCOUTS OF
CENTRAL MARYLAND

A Tree for the Future

By Juliette Gordon Low

Every spring
The sap rises in the trees
From root to branch
And makes a tree that looks dead
Blossom with green leaves
And life.
So it is that the Scouting Spirit
Rises within you and
Inspires you to put forth
Your best.

On the Cover: Service has always been the cornerstone of the Girl Scout program. During World War II, Girl Scouts engaged in activities supporting the armed services and were known as Senior Service Troops. Shown riding down Charles Street in Baltimore City, a Girl Scout trains for duty as a bicycle messenger. (Girl Scouts of Central Maryland Archives Committee.)

IMAGES
of America

GIRL SCOUTS OF
CENTRAL MARYLAND

Roberta F. Dorsch on behalf of the
Girl Scouts of Central Maryland

ARCADIA
PUBLISHING

Copyright © 2012 by Roberta F. Dorsch on behalf of the Girl Scouts of Central Maryland
ISBN 978-0-7385-9234-3

Published by Arcadia Publishing
Charleston, South Carolina

Printed in the United States of America

Library of Congress Control Number: 2011941626

For all general information, please contact Arcadia Publishing:
Telephone 843-853-2070
Fax 843-853-0044
E-mail sales@arcadiapublishing.com
For customer service and orders:
Toll-Free 1-888-313-2665

Visit us on the Internet at www.arcadiapublishing.com

*This book is dedicated to Juliette Gordon Low and all
of the Girl Guides and Girl Scouts, past, present, and
future, who live out their dreams every day.*

CONTENTS

ACKNOWLEDGMENTS

When I had the idea of creating this book I knew that it would require the assistance of many people. The cooperation I received made this book possible and enjoyable. First, I want to thank the leadership of the Girl Scouts of Central Maryland (GSCM), particularly chief executive officer Traci Barnett, for allowing me to undertake this project and for their support in the production of this history of the council. Danita Terry, the GSCM director of communications, assisted with gathering photographs and information and with editing. Marcia (Johnson) Darby, the GSCM vice president of advancement, also was helpful with editing. Thanks also to the members of the GSCM Archives Committee for their suggestions and support.

The majority of the information and pictures included in this collection came from the archives of the GSCM, however there were many troop leaders and adult Girl Scouts—such as Lucy Marshall, Mary Jo Robl, and Carol Wier—who provided pictures and personal memories of Scouting activities. Unless otherwise noted, the photographs used were reproduced from the collections maintained by the GSCM Archives Committee. A special thank-you to Lifetime Girl Scout and active supporter Sen. Barbara Mikulski for her time and participation in this project.

Thanks also to my friends and family who provided much encouragement along with their help. Special thanks to my daughter Brenda Ibutu (a Girl Scout Gold Award recipient and Lifetime Member) and my son-in-law Timothy Ibutu for helping put all of the material together and for help with editing, and to my husband Dennis (a Thanks Badge recipient and Lifetime Member), who not only helped with gathering information and editing but also dealt with doing cooking and cleaning during this long project.

No history of Girl Scouting could fail to acknowledge the work and leadership of Juliette Gordon Low. My own years as a young Girl Scout (a Curved Bar recipient and Lifetime Member) led me to love Girl Scouting and to become a leader. I am grateful for the opportunity to share this history with past, present, and future Girl Scouts throughout the Girl Scouts of Central Maryland and beyond.

INTRODUCTION

After returning home to Georgia from England in 1912, Juliette Gordon Low placed what became a historic telephone call to her cousin Nina Anderson Pape: "Come right over! I've got something for the girls of Savannah, and all of America, and all the world, and we're going to start it tonight!" They set about a spirited campaign to raise interest and enlist girls, mothers, and leaders throughout Savannah from every social, economic, and religious strata into her American Girl Guide organization. On March 12, 1912, Juliette gathered and registered 18 girls, forming America's first female Scouting troop, and called them American Girl Guides. Based on her experiences in Europe, Juliette knew that girls in the United States would also jump at a chance to participate in fun activities such as outdoor experiences, service to others, and citizenship.

Juliette Magill Kinzie Gordon was born on October 31, 1860, in Savannah, Georgia. Known as "Daisy" to family and friends, she was the second of six children born to a family of wealth and distinction. Her father, William Washington Gordon II, was a high-ranking Confederate officer who made a fortune in the cotton trade. He became a general in the Spanish-American War. Juliette's mother, Eleanor Lytle (Kinzie) Gordon, was from one of Chicago's founding families. Eleanor authored a book chronicling her father's adventures and experiences as a government agent working among Native Americans on the Western frontier.

In 1864, at the age of four, Juliette and her sisters were sent to live with her maternal grandparents in Chicago, far from the strife and danger prevailing in Savannah toward the end of the Civil War. To the youthful Juliette, tales of her grandfather's frontier experiences were immensely appealing. She grew to be an active and sociable child, playing outdoor games and horseback riding. She loved animals of every kind, especially birds, and from an early age she developed a love of the arts and wrote plays and poetry. Juliette spent many summers with her sisters and cousins at an aunt's estate in north Georgia. There, her love of camping and hunting emerged, in addition to hikes in the woods, canoeing, and the occasional practical joke.

Juliette was educated in prominent boarding schools in Georgia, Virginia, and New Jersey, and she attended a French finishing school in Manhattan. She studied dramatic writing and painting. She toured Europe after completing her education, where she began a four-year courtship with William Mackay Low, a wealthy British landowner and cotton merchant, who also had family and business ties to Savannah. When she was about 25 years old, Juliette developed an ear infection that was treated with silver nitrate. The experimental treatment damaged her ear and resulted in significant hearing loss.

In 1886, Juliette and William were married in Savannah. During the ceremony, a grain of wedding rice lodged in Juliette's healthy ear and became infected. When the doctor attempted to remove the rice, it damaged nerves and caused total deafness in that ear. For the rest of her life, Juliette used various hearing aids. The couple lived in Scotland and London and traveled extensively, returning to America yearly to visit relatives. The couple never had children, and in the years before her husband's death in 1905, the marriage was unhappy.

By 1911, at age 51, Juliette's social circle in England brought her into contact with Sir Robert Baden-Powell, who had founded the Boy Scouts organization. The two became good friends, and Baden-Powell introduced Juliette to his sister Agnes, who, with him, had founded a similar group for girls known as the Girl Guides. The social aims of the Boy Scouts and Girl Guides—to provide healthy activities for children while instilling a sense of responsible citizenship—struck a chord in Juliette. She soon founded her own Girl Guide troops in Scotland and England. Her enthusiasm for the cause quickly evolved into a desire to introduce the Girl Guides program in the United States.

In 1912, Juliette established a group that included two small troops of girls who met in the carriage house behind her Savannah home. The Girl Guides engaged in a variety of sports and outdoor activities including camping. Other girls in Savannah were eager to join in the fun, and the response convinced Juliette that a nationwide organization should be formed. Margaret (Daisy Doots) Gordon, Juliette's niece, was the first registered member. Juliette's mother, Eleanor, was a "guide mistress" (now "troop leader").

In 1913, the name Girl Guides was changed to the Girl Scouts of the United States. That same year, a group of women in Pikesville, Maryland, decided to form a chapter in their area. They sent a letter to Sir Baden-Powell requesting information about the Girl Guides organization. In May, they received a response from Juliette's secretary, followed by a handbook, and thus began the first Girl Scout troop in the Baltimore area. Under the leadership of Bolling Barton, this troop, which was the 11th in the country, promptly adopted the name Poppy troop. Their charter, signed by Juliette, is in safe storage at the Central Maryland archives. In 1914, the Pansy Patrol troop became Baltimore City's first Girl Scout troop. By 1915, the Girl Scout organization was incorporated, with national headquarters in Washington, DC. "Daisy" Low served as the first president until 1920. In 1916, the Girl Scout Council of Baltimore and Baltimore County was organized, and Bolling Barton served as the commissioner/president. There were already more than 7,000 girls enrolled in the Girl Scouts across the country.

On March 6, 1928, the Baltimore Area Girl Scout Council, Inc., was incorporated as a non-stock corporation. The Anne Arundel County Girl Scout Council, Inc., was incorporated on June 19, 1940, and the Frederick County Girl Scout Council was incorporated on April 28, 1958. The consolidation of the three councils took place on October 1, 1962, forming the Girl Scouts of Central Maryland, with a girl membership of almost 25,000 and more than 6,500 adult members. It was also the 50th anniversary of the Girl Scouts of the United States. C. Lease Bussard served as the organizing president of the new council for two months and was followed by Ruth Gore.

Currently, Girls Scouts of the United States and Girl Guides across the world have 10 million members in 145 countries. Over the decades, Girl Scouting has flourished to serve more than 50 million American women and continues to be a way for girls to explore the world around them and learn new skills for the future. Girl Scouts of Central Maryland (GSCM) has grown along with the national organization, enriching the lives of many prominent women over the years.

One

GIRL SCOUTING BLOOMS POPPIES AND PANSIES

The Girl Scouts of Central Maryland (GSCM) and the Girl Scouts of the United States of America (GSUSA) share important milestones in the year 2012: the 50-year and 100-year anniversary celebrations, respectively. Nationally, it began when Juliette Gordon Low brought to Savannah a Scouting program for girls, modeled after the one begun by Lord Robert Baden-Powell in England. In Pikesville, Maryland, Bolling Barton heard about Girl Guides and promptly wrote Powell a letter requesting information for starting a chapter in Baltimore for a group of acquaintances. She received correspondence from Low and a charter for a group called the Poppy troop in 1913; it was the 11th club nationally. In 1914, the Pansy Patrol troop was organized and chartered in Baltimore City. Using her business and personal connections, Low continued to mobilize like-minded women, such as Lou Henry Hoover and Edith Macy. With help from these and other committed women, the Scouting program rapidly spread across the country.

Many current activities associated with Girl Scouts were also present in the beginning years. Camping was very popular, which led to the formation of several resident camps in the 1920s. Camp Whippoorwill, on the Magothy River, opened in Anne Arundel County in 1928. Camp Woodlands, in Annapolis on the Broad River, was acquired in 1944 and is distinguished by having a Teepee building, a structure resembling the 12-sided polygonal units used by Native Americans. The main area of this structure was designed by Charles Lamb, son of Anne Arundel County Council commissioner Ruth Lamb. The Teepee building received national acclaim when it was awarded the American Institute of Architects Certificate of Merit in 1954.

While the style of uniforms and badges has changed, Scouts continue to wear with pride their sashes, vests, and earned badges. Over the years, the name of the highest achievable award in Girl Scouts has changed several times, but the challenge of earning it has not. Name changes from the original 1916 Golden Eagle Merit have included the 1919 Golden Eaglet Award, 1922 Order of the Gold Eagle, 1938 First Class, 1940 Curved Bar, 1963 First Class, and 1980 Gold Award. In 1996, the national board resolved to retain the Gold Award name from that period forward.

No. 11

CERTIFICATE

GIRL SCOUTS

HEADQUARTERS: WASHINGTON, D. C.

This Certifies that _Elsie L. Barton_ has received the approval of the National Headquarters of the Girl Scouts, and is hereby duly appointed Scout Captain of _Poppy_ Troop of the City of _Roslyn_ State of _Maryland_.

Issued this _10th_ day of _October_ 1913.

Juliette Low

EXECUTIVE

This certificate shows the first charter issued to the Baltimore area, Poppy troop, in 1913. The troop was chartered to Roslyn, although it is listed through the GSCM as Pikesville. It was the 11th troop in the United States. Also, in 1913, Low established the national headquarters in Washington, DC, where it remained until 1916 when it moved to New York City. In 1915, the organization was officially incorporated, and Low held the position of president for five years. Over the years, there was significant growth in the Baltimore area. Anne Arundel County was also very active, as were Baltimore City, Baltimore County, and Frederick and Harford Counties.

Mr. and Mrs. Coghlan of Pikesville, who also volunteered as managers and supporters of the Girl Scouts, donated a house, known as the Scout Club House. The clubhouse was used as a gathering spot for the girls to work on activities such as cooking, sewing, knot tying, and outdoor skills. Having their own meeting place made the girls feel special. It also added to the excitement of this new opportunity for girls of all ages.

Members of the Poppy troop (Troop 3, Pikesville) stand in front of the Scout Club House, where they held meetings. They were followed by a troop in Baltimore City. The girls were recruited at rallies in various parts of Baltimore City.

The adventure of camping has long been a part of the Girl Scout experience. These girls' bags are packed, and they are ready for an exciting week at Camp Bradley, located on the grounds of Aberdeen Proving Grounds. The adult counselors and camp director were trained at Camp Bradley before the girls arrived.

Around 1920, Camp Bradley, at Aberdeen Proving Ground, cost $6.00 per week. The Baltimore and Washington, DC, councils held the camp jointly, as there were not enough girls in either council to attend individually. Military personnel pitched tents and created pathways so that the girls could get around, even in bad weather.

Girl Scouts were accustomed to being awakened by a bugle each morning. Some troops still uphold this tradition. Other traditions continued include respect for the flag and wearing the Girl Scout uniform.

These girls are showing off their camp uniforms and a patrol flag as they prepare to show visitors around the camp. Campers were not permitted to receive packages of food of any kind, a policy still in place; they went to the canteen each day. Activities included hiking, swimming, and outdoor sports.

In the 1920s, the camps did not have buildings with fully equipped kitchens. These girls set up camp with an area for cooking and washing. During this period, all meals were cooked outdoors, over the campfire. Camps today may have fully equipped kitchens, but the girls still cook over the campfire and use mesh kits that hold their dishes and utensils.

Kaper charts are used by all troops to list the duties assigned to each girl. The charts are used during camping trips and at troop meetings to help assign responsibilities. These Scouts from about 1950 are learning their camp schedule. At this time, African American girls camped in Pasadena, Maryland, and at Camp Woodlands in Annapolis. By 1954, camps were fully integrated.

Dinnertime is near, and kaper duty for these girls must have been corn shucking for their friends. There were no dining halls or cooks. Everything was prepared over a campfire. Uniforms at the time included loose tunic tops and knee-high socks.

While camp clothing has certainly changed, the tradition of taking photographs with friends in front of one's tent remains. These girls at Camp Bradley show that music and singing have always been popular among Girl Scouts.

Girls are pictured working on a sewing or craft project. While they worked diligently, kaper projects often made way for more enjoyable activities.

Girls at Camp Conowingo's Chimney Trail take time out of their day in the morning and evening to honor the country with a formal flag ceremony. At that time, girls saluted the flag at formal attention; while girls now may not do that, there is still a formal flag ceremony at the beginning and end of each meeting.

In this c. 1920 photograph, girls at Camp Bradley prepare for a night of singing and fun, with their campfire ready to light. They may have prepared group skits or songs relaying activities they did during their time at camp. Songs around a campfire are part of what binds campers together in the past and the present.

Once the skits and s'mores are finished, it is time to sing a few more songs as the flames turn to embers.

An early troop marches in a parade in Baltimore around 1915, proudly waving their patrol flag. Parades have always been and continue to be a favorite Girl Scout activity and a way that girls honor their country.

Shown here, the Baltimore Area council holds a rally at Western High School. Recruitment rallies brought in new members, both girls and adult volunteers. In the early years, they were council events. But, over time and with increasing membership, the rallies became local or unit rallies.

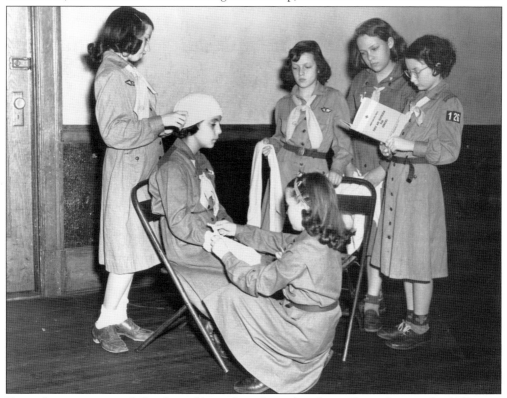

First-aid training was a skill girls could use throughout their lives. Shown here in the 1950s, two girls practice bandaging an injured person as an interim step before a doctor arrives. During the war years, proficiency in first aid was considered an especially important life skill among Girl Scouts.

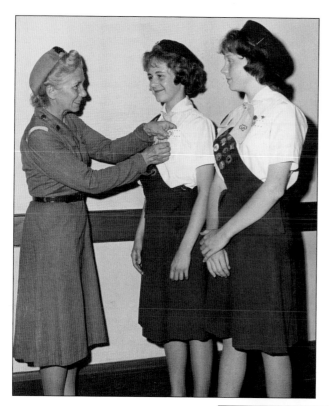

Each year, Girl Scouts work hard to earn badges and honors. Shown here, the annual Court of Awards ceremony takes place, and the troop's leader, or a council representative, presents the girls with their awards for that year.

Over the years, the Annapolis and Baltimore Area Girl Scout councils were located in nine different offices. In the beginning, the office was a single room; as the council grew, so did the need for a larger office. This office, in the Singley building at the Keswick Home in Roland Park, was used from 1976 through 1996, until construction of today's office at 4806 Seton Drive was complete.

Adele De Leeuw (right) and Margaret Dudley cowrote *The Rugged Dozen Abroad* in the 1950s, based on the experiences of taking a Towson, Maryland, senior Girl Scout troop on an 11-week tour of Europe. The girls boarded a ship to England and met Girl Guides, the Scouting counterparts from European countries.

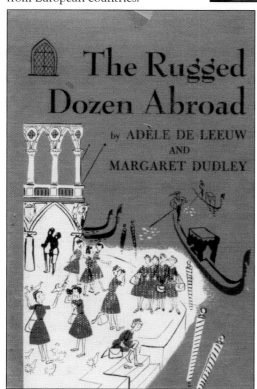

For many years, the Baltimore department store Hochschild-Kohn was the place where people went for their Girl Scout uniforms and other Scouting goods. The window display shown here was placed for a week to mark the 40th anniversary of GSUSA.

Photographed in 1962, the three past presidents from the former councils that merged to become the Girl Scouts of Central Maryland are, from left to right, Gail Bunting from Anne Arundel County, Margaret Waldschmidt from the Baltimore area; and Fran Lease Bussard from Frederick County.

Two

FOR EVERY GIRL, EVERYWHERE

GSCM offers a variety of programs and events each year that encourage the development of courage, confidence, and character in all girls. The traditional activities provide not only fun and friendship but also opportunities for girls to develop useful lifelong skills. From the time a girl turns five, she is able to become a Girl Scout. There are six levels, all of which are considered Girl Scouts. Daisy Girl Scouts are usually in kindergarten. Brownie Girl Scouts are ages 6 to 8, Junior Girl Scouts are ages 9 to 12, Cadette Girl Scouts are ages 13 to 14, Senior Girl Scouts are ages 15 and 16, and Ambassador Girl Scouts are ages 17 to 18. From the age of 18, women—and men—are able to volunteer or become staff members in various capacities.

In addition to providing traditional Scouting pursuits, GSCM offers outreach programs for nontraditional Girl Scout troops and groups that meet in locations such as alternative schools and inner-city community centers. The programs were developed to provide all girls access to Girl Scouting activities and benefits, as described in more detail below.

The Beyond Bars program supports girls whose mothers are incarcerated. The goals of the program are to help reduce children's trauma surrounding incarceration while mitigating intergenerational incarceration and to increase parenting skills during and after incarceration while promoting the mother-child bond. The program has been recognized by several state and national justice organizations. Since it was piloted by the GSCM, more than 50 Girl Scout councils have implemented the program.

The GSCM chapter initiated another nationally recognized program. Called the Project Anti-Violence Education (PAVE) program, it empowers high school teens to mentor elementary and middle-school children by giving them leadership training. Then, the PAVE teen mentors develop programs that help younger, at-risk children build the courage, confidence, and character to resist the negative influences of bullying and gang interactions in favor of choices that can assure their successful development into young women. The program leverages young children's natural inclination to admire and emulate the actions of older children. PAVE teen mentors also develop and implement a weeklong summer day camp for elementary and middle school children.

A number of travel opportunities are available for Girl Scouts in their teens via GSCM's Destinations program, formerly known as Wider Opportunities. Held in various states and abroad, it allows girls to engage in the in-depth study of a chosen topic such as sightseeing, canoeing, or scuba diving. In 2004, GSCM sponsored a Wider Opportunities effort that involved sailing a tall ship, called "Chesapeake Challenge: Sail a Tall Ship." Other GSCM members have traveled to Costa Rica, Alaska, and Alabama through the Destinations program.

Harvest for the Hungry is an ongoing initiative that provides food to local food banks. Collaborating with the Maryland Food Bank, which collects and distributes food to thousands of Maryland families and individuals; GSCM has participated in the program since 1997.

Pres. C. Lease Bussard signs the new council's charter issued by GSUSA. Looking on is Ruth Gore, president-elect. The consolidation of the three councils took place on October 1, 1962. The first GSCM office address was 128 West Franklin Street. The original charter granted authority to develop, manage, and maintain Girl Scouting in six surrounding Maryland counties and Baltimore City through 1964.

Margaret Waldschmidt, GSCM council president, announces upcoming Scouting events by radio broadcast sometime around 1959.

Photographed at GSCM Council headquarters are, from left to right, Girl Scout Research Institute Senior Advocacy vice president Laurie Westley, GSCM chief executive officer Traci Barnett, GSUSA National Board chair Connie Lindsey, and GSCM vice president of advancement Maria (Johnson) Darby. The gathering marked the 100th-anniversary kickoff event to honor Sen. Barbara Mikulski (D-MD), a lifetime Girl Scout, for her congressional support of the Girl Scouts.

Shown here around 2010 are those who attended the Distinguished Women's Award reception, GSCM's annual fundraiser, which began in 1981. The event honors local businesswomen who have achieved outstanding professional and civic accomplishments. Over the years, honorees have included Helen Amos in 2003, Floraine Applefeld in 1984, C. Sylvia Brown in 2003, Ethel Ennis in 1981, Bea Gaddy in 1992, the Honorable Irma Raker in 1999, Mary Pat Seurkamp in 2006, Pam Shriver in 1981, and Ellen Yankellow in 2010.

Adults receive many awards from the GSCM council and their peers, including the Appreciation Pin, Honor Pin, Thanks Badge I, and Thanks Badge II. Shown here, GSCM president Sandra McNeal (left) presents a Thanks Badge to volunteer Carol Wier. When the Thanks Badge was first used in 1912, it was awarded to non–Girl Scout adults to whom the council or a service unit owed gratitude for promoting Girl Scouting. Beginning in 1987, the purpose changed to honor Girl Scout members whose service goes significantly beyond the call of duty.

Pictured from left to right are Cassandra Moore (mother of Laura); Laura Moore, GSCM's first Gold Award Young Woman of Distinction; Veronica Koch Kelly; and Patricia Tracey—both members of GSCM's Gold Award Committee. The Gold Award Young Woman of Distinction is a special honor given by GSUSA to girls whose Gold Award project is deemed worthy of this special recognition. After earning the Gold Award, Laura went on to study pre-law and Latin at the University of Richmond on a full scholarship. Her Gold Award project was designed to help minority families prepare their children for college preparatory courses. This idea was adopted by the Anne Arundel County school system. Laura was the keynote speaker at the 2006 Gold Award banquet.

Alex Dunbar presents a check to representatives of GSCM to honor the memory of his daughter Caitlin, a Girl Scout who loved nature and the outdoors. She died from a rare form of leukemia. The first Caitlin Dunbar Nature Center was at Camp Conowingo. A second Caitlin Dunbar Nature Center was later opened at Camp Ilchester.

The Caitlin Dunbar Nature Center, shown here was created in 2006 at Camp Conowingo in Cecil County, Maryland. There is also a small bronze statue, symbolizing Caitlin, for whom the nature center was named.

The Caitlin Dunbar Nature Center includes a spacious deck that has provided a quiet place for Scouts to relax, spend free time, or enjoy nature activities. Much of the construction work was done by Caitlin's parents, friends, Girl Scouts, and a local Boy Scout.

The Caitlin Dunbar Nature Centers at both Camps Conowingo and Ilchester have murals along the walls, all painted by various Girl Scout troops. Caitlin spent 10 consecutive summers at Camp Conowingo during her brief life.

The nature center features a variety of aquariums and tanks that enable Scouts to study the resident animals up close, including a working bee hive (right).

Girl Scouts pose around the state seal in the Maryland Statehouse in Annapolis during Maryland Girl Scouts Legislative Day.

These Girl Scouts were able to connect with Gov. Martin O'Malley during Legislative Day 2008. The day is set aside for older Girl Scouts statewide to meet in Annapolis with their legislators, attend a hearing or a legislative session, and take part in other experiences in the historic city.

During Legislative Day 2011, Troop 1921 formed. It was the first Honorary Maryland Women Legislative Girl Scout Troop. State senator Katherine Klausmeier (below left), state senator Nancy Jacobs (above left), state delegate Adrienne Jones, and delegate Gail Bates served as cochairs.

Mayor Theodore McKeldin (Baltimore City) signs a Girl Scout Week proclamation, as three Girl Scouts bear witness.

Gov. Parris Glendening presents a state of Maryland Girl Scout Week proclamation to local Girl Scouts.

Local Girl Scouts join Gov. William Donald Schaefer to celebrate the signing of Maryland's first statewide Protection Bill on April 30, 1991. As part of the ceremony, a five-foot Liberty elm tree was planted on the state house's northern lawn. This disease-resistant hybrid tree could grow to 80 feet during a person's lifetime. An estimated 1.4 million trees were distributed by state and local nurseries during Earth Month in 1991.

Girl Scouts pose with Maryland state senator Lisa Gladden, a sponsor of bond bill legislation to provide initial funding for GSCM's headquarters expansion.

County executive Dennis F. Rasmussen is photographed helping Girl Scouts celebrate their 75th anniversary by declaring March 23–29 Girl Scouts Week in Baltimore County. The GSUSA is the world's largest voluntary organization dedicated to teaching girls leadership skills they will use for a lifetime.

Girl Scouts were invited to city hall in 2010 to participate in the flag procession of the Baltimore Black Heritage Festival's opening ceremony. Mayor Stephanie Rawlings-Blake issued the invitation for all Girl Scouts to attend.

The Girl Scout cookie kickoff was held at the Howard County Fairgrounds. There were stations set up for the girls to visit, including face-painting, sale safety instructions, and cookie booth marketing ideas.

These girls show they are ready to sell cookies after getting tips at this cookie rally. Girls who sold at least 500 boxes received invitations to the council's 500+ Club celebration.

To get girls excited and prepared for the upcoming cookie sale, celebrities such as Tony the Tiger and the Keebler Elf made special appearances.

Pictured are graduates of GSCM's first Cookie College, a financial literacy activity aimed at preparing girls for the cookie program. This program is one of many activities that take place to sharpen girls' sales and public-relation skills.

Troops sell Girl Scout cookies door-to-door to neighbors and friends. Some also set up cookie booths and get very creative with posters to attract people who are shopping in nearby stores.

Frances Hesselbein (pictured above and below) began her Girl Scout career as a troop leader in Western Pennsylvania and eventually became a part of the state's Girl Scout leadership team. Her success caught the attention of the national Girl Scout organization, and she soon became CEO of GSUSA. While there, she implemented the philosophies of management guru Peter Drucker. Later, she went on to work for Drucker, managing his Leader-to-Leader Institute. In 2007, Hesselbein was the featured guest at GSCM's first Women's Leadership Forum held in the Wheeler Auditorium of the Enoch Pratt Library in Baltimore City. She shared success stories, management tips, and leadership approaches with nearly 200 guests. Hesselbein has stayed connected to the girls and enjoyed meeting a Brownie Girl Scout and her Cookie Monster in the above image.

The Green Carpet event celebrates girls who sell the most cookies during the preorder phase of the annual Girl Scout cookie sale. The 2008 top sellers shown here arrived in limousines and were the designated stars for the evening. Local chefs Nancy Longo, owner of Pierpoint Restaurant and Catering, and Duff Goldman, of Charm City Cakes and the *Ace of Cakes* television show, prepared Girl Scout cookie–inspired dishes for guests. The Food Network filmed the event for an episode of *Ace of Cakes*. Longo revealed that cooking at Camp Conowingo as a young Girl Scout sparked her culinary interest. Pictured below are Ann Quassman, host of *Woman Talk Live* (WCBM), Duff Goldman, and Miss Teen Maryland.

Photographed in 2008, chef Duff Goldman and chef Nancy Longo make final preparations for the Green Carpet event.

For two years, Food Network's *Ace of Cakes* and Baltimore's own Duff Goldman, owner of Charm City Cakes, provided an array of beautifully decorated cakes for the GSCM Green Carpet event.

Girls line up for a piece of the gorgeous cake that Duff Goldman created. The *Ace of Cakes* star is known for his inspired cake decorations.

These Girl Scouts each sold at least 500 boxes of cookies during the annual Girl Scout cookie sale and earned membership in the 500+ Club. Their hard work and dedication earned them a private meeting with entertainers from the Ringling Bros. and Barnum & Bailey Circus at First Mariner Arena.

Around 2008, these 500+ Club girls enjoyed a backstage meeting with clowns and other circus performers before the show. The highlight for many was meeting the ringmaster (below), one of the few female ringmasters in the circus community.

The first council-sponsored World Thinking Day took place in 2006 at Wilde Lake High School in Howard County. World Thinking Day is designed to connect Girl Scouts and Girl Guides across the globe. It features cultural dance, art, food, games, and displays representing various countries in the World Association of Girl Guides and Girl Scouts (WAGGGS). The event in 2006 was brought about with the help of Girl Scout Troop 2701.

As part of World Thinking Day, Girl Scouts observe cultural dancing, demonstrated above by ethnic Indian Dancers and below by a Korean Dance and Drums ensemble.

These girls had an opportunity to play international games and learn international dances at the council-sponsored World Thinking Day at the 2006 event. Many Girl Scout troops plan and create World Thinking Day events in their service units or with other troops.

The Lady Maryland/Girl Scout Inner City Sail project was an exciting venture for 30 girls who lived in Baltimore City. They sailed several times during the week and learned key sailing skills, including steering, navigating, tying knots, controlling sails, water chemistry, and deck swabbing. The girls also sang songs and learned the history of the Chesapeake Bay pungy schooner *Lady Maryland*. This image was taken in the late 1980s or early 1990s.

Girl Scouts, baseball, and camping combined to form a new twist on classic American traditions. Shown here, Girl Scouts prepare for an overnight encampment at Ripken Stadium in Harford County. This outing provided an enjoyable variation on the traditional camping venue.

Shown here, local Girl Scouts were invited to attend a Baltimore Orioles game, as part of Girl Scout night at Camden Yards. While there, the girls participated in activities that helped them earn a patch. It was great to see them on the Jumbotron. Girl Scouts also performed the opening flag ceremony.

When the Nickelodeon television network challenged children to turn off the television and "get out and play," local Girl Scout Autumn Johnson received an award for her healthy lifestyle submission. She received funds to host a Day of Play at Camp Ilchester for her friends and troop members (below). Pictured above around 2007, from left to right, are Howard County delegate Shane Pendergrass, Autumn Johnson, GSCM chief executive officer Traci Barnett, and troop leader Clarissa Ferraris.

The National Mall in Washington, DC, has been the site for Girl Scout sing-alongs since the 85th anniversary of the Girl Scouts in 1997. Held every five years, members gather from many states to participate in the anniversary celebrations. It was exhilarating for the girls to see and be a part of this "sea of Girl Scouts" that gathered together in a common bond. Central Maryland troops participated and had a wonderful time.

The GSCM chorus performs at many Girl Scout events. Pat Disharoon, photographed here with the accordion, has served as the leader of the group for many years. For this performance, choristers were attired in Girl Scout uniforms from days past. Mary McClurg, GSCM board chair, stands at the far left.

Cantastic is a program that provides canned goods and other nonperishables to local food pantries. The girls are challenged to build various structures. This troop built the Lincoln Memorial. After the display event takes place, the canned items are delivered to local food banks.

GSCM's first Wider Opportunities event, held in 2004, was the "Chesapeake Challenge . . . Sail a Tall Ship," which drew participants from 17 states and Australia. The Girl Scouts took a 10-day voyage that gave them a taste of 19th-century sailing life. While aboard a 72-foot Chesapeake Bay pungy schooner, girls tended sails, stood watch, and plotted the vessel's course to a number of ports of call along the bay. Wider Opportunities programs, now called Destinations, are designed to allow girls to explore outside of their council region, state, or country.

Girl Scouts along with their troop members and families converge at Camp Whippoorwill to participate in the Cardboard Boat Regatta. The challenge was to make a boat out of cardboard and compete against other Girl Scouts to see whose boat could stay afloat the longest or sink the fastest. For their boat, the team with the bubble wrap, above, used critical thinking and chutzpah. Some boats did not get far; those girls took a swim, as shown below.

Girl Scout Sunday/Sabbath is a nationwide event marking the beginning of Girl Scout Week. The event takes place at many houses of worship throughout the council area. The girls at right stand before the cathedral of Mary Our Queen in Baltimore City. Below, GSCM executive director Beverly Gayhart is seated at the right front.

Members of Girl Scout Troop 913 from Edgewater, Maryland, are on hand at the ground-breaking for the Butterfly Boutique, a project associated with the troop's Gold Award projects. With community help, the girls implemented a plan to create a resale store on the grounds of the Chrysallis House in Anne Arundel County. The boutique is used to train residents and to generate income for the addiction rehabilitation center.

During this Girl Scout aquatic expedition, Scouts searched for artifacts along the shoreline then spent time examining and researching the specimens they uncovered.

The Girl Scouts Beyond Bars program began in 1992 as a partnership between GSCM and the National Institute of Justice. The program ensures that this troop of girls shares regular visits with their mothers, who are incarcerated at the Maryland Correctional Institute for Women in Jessup. With supervision and guidance from GSCM staff members, the mothers and daughters participate in traditional troop activities. Literacy training is available. Another program counsels and empowers girls to resist negative peer pressure. The Beyond Bars program has been adopted by other Girl Scout councils. It has been effective in improving positive decision-making and nurturing the bond between mothers and daughters. Above, local actress Maria Broom poses after leading a self-esteem experience. Below, a member of the troop describes the positive impact of the program.

The Girl Scout Gold Award is the highest award a Girl Scout can earn. Gold Award projects take careful planning and preparation. To receive a Gold Award, a Girl Scout must implement a sustainable project in the community. In addition to the many skills gained—including team work and community relations—girls are awarded college scholarships for the completion of this prestigious award.

This Girl Scout is reciting the Girl Scout Promise as she receives the coveted Girl Scout Gold Award at the council-wide banquet. To earn it, a girl must demonstrate expertise in several areas of Girl Scouting and complete a major project. Many troops hold their own Court of Awards ceremony to share their accomplishments with family and friends, in addition to the council event. Recipients demonstrate expertise in project management and implementation to complete the project.

Bell Manor is a 19th-century mansion nestled along the Susquehanna River in Cecil County, Maryland. GSCM acquired the property in 1961, along with the 300 acres surrounding the ornate mansion, it is part of Camp Conowingo. By the early 2000s, time and wear had taken a toll, and the building was in need of major repair, including the slate roof. The Friends of Bell Manor committee decided to sell the old slates, which they decorated with various designs, to raise money for the necessary repairs.

It took several years to renovate Bell Manor. Restoring the mansion to its original beauty took investments in time and money. Windows were replaced and restored, Italianate corbels were painted and protected from the elements, and floors were refurbished or replaced to their original beauty. In 2008, GSCM held a grand reopening to celebrate the mansion's restoration.

Girl Scouts love to camp. Nothing can stop them. This troop arrived at camp in time for a rainy weekend. Undaunted by the drizzle, these campers move forward with the standard program, including cooking and enjoying time by the campfire.

The Chesapeake Bay has been an integral part of Girl Scouting in Central Maryland. This girl holds a crab that washed up on shore. It could have been a delicious treat.

Three

A Sister to Every Girl Scout

Through the years, GSUSA has held to the ideals set forth in the Girl Scout Promise and Law. While growing up, Girl Scouts at all levels enjoy the same kinds of activities: serving their community, earning badges, going to camp, enjoying friendships, and learning life skills. As they get older, girls are able to explore the world farther away from home and take on projects that are progressively more challenging and that have a more lasting impact on the world around them.

Juliette Gordon Low understood the importance of recognition ceremonies to honor the actions and achievements of all members; this tradition has been in place since the Girl Scout organization began. Girls earn badges and pins on the troop level, often as a group, but some also earn special recognitions for their service to others, usually outside of the troop setting. The Golden Eagle of Merit was the highest award in Girl Scouting from 1916 to 1919. In 1980, the Gold Award was introduced, replacing earlier versions.

Girl Scout Juniors and Cadettes are able to work together or individually on the Bronze and Silver Award, by completing community projects that help prepare them for their work on the Gold Award. To earn the highest award, a Senior or Ambassador Girl Scout must develop and implement a sustainable project that benefits not only her, but also her community.

All adult members are eligible to receive recognition for volunteer service that goes above and beyond standard duty. There are four badges used. The Thanks Badge rewards an original or specific volunteer service or act. The Thanks Badge II, originating in 1987, rewards continuing or additional meritorious service. The Appreciation Pin was first introduced in 1976, and it recognizes exceptional leadership service. Also introduced in 1976, the Honor Pin recognizes exemplary leadership service in two or more geographic areas.

While Girl Scouts are earning badges and learning about themselves and their fellow Girl Scouts and Girl Guides around the world, they are having fun! Some events are unique to individual troops while others happen on both a council and/or troop level, providing even more exciting opportunities.

Pictured in the 1970s, GSCM staff member Maria (Darby) Johnson shared a photograph of her Bridging Ceremony at St. Mary's of the Assumption Roman Catholic Church in Baltimore. Often using candles, the Bridging Ceremony is an opportunity for Girl Scouts to renew their commitment to the Girl Scout Promise and Law.

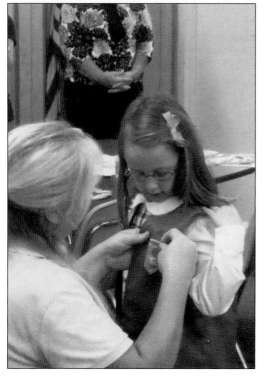

A Daisy Girl Scout is being invested as a member of the Girl Scouts during the Investiture Ceremony. She looks on as she receives her first Girl Scout pins. After she is welcomed into Girl Scouting, she recites the Girl Scout Promise and Law.

During the 1950s, there were Girl Scout Roundups in various parts of the country. Troops were able to participate, along with their leaders. This troop, with leader Edna Merson, prepares to leave for Detroit, where it joined other Scouts to participate in a variety of Girl Scout activities, such as camping and hiking.

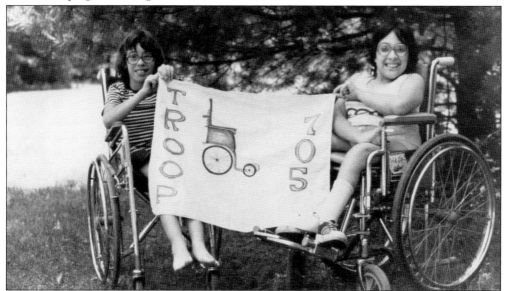

Girl Scouting welcomes the participation of girls of all abilities. Here, girls from Troop 705 display their troop's signage at camp in the 1950s.

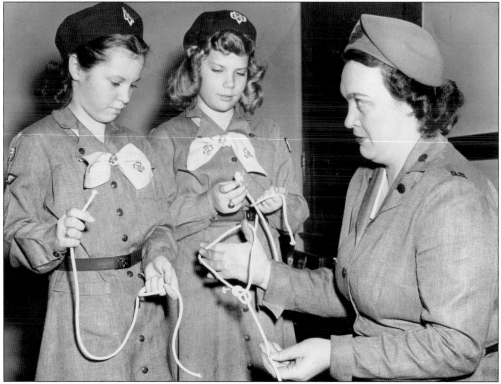

These girls are learning to tie different kinds of knots, a very useful skill when camping and boating. Pitching a tent correctly requires the right knot, something one does not want to learn during a heavy storm.

An all-time favorite in Central Maryland is a tractor ride through the Naval Academy farm.

A local expert teaches this young Girl Scout some of the skills needed to perform archeological excavations. Here, they filter dirt through a sieve to capture hidden artifacts.

During the 1950s and 1960s, writing letters to distant or foreign pen-pal friends was popular among girls. Many Girl Scout troops also established correspondence with girls from other countries. It was a clever way to learn how many others across the world spent their lives—an antecedent to today's Facebook. Through this cultural exchange, traditions, language, games, and dances of other countries were also shared.

This Mariner troop left on a cruise to Norfolk, Virginia, on the *Gray Goose*, a schooner yacht belonging to Capt. F.J. Watcott. Mariner Scouts, whose activities focused on seafaring, worked long and hard to prepare for the sea voyage. These girls wave farewell to friends and relatives as they set sail from the Baltimore Harbor.

Gwen Burdett, a Mariner Girl Scout, poses in 1971 in her formal uniform and white groves. Her ship was No. 40.

These girls invite new members to join up and make sure passers-by see how much fun they are having. What a great recruitment tool! Troops are very creative and resourceful in showing other girls where the fun is.

Girl Scout troops often open and close their meetings with a Friendship Circle, shown here by these Brownies.

Brownies use the Brownie Ring forum, shown here, to make decisions and divide tasks and activities. Older girls use the Patrol System.

After troop business is resolved, it is time for fun. Here, girls use the Brownie Ring to play Duck, Duck, Goose.

Learning the proper way to handle the American flag is an important task in Girl Scouting. At troop meetings, girls are often responsible for lowering the flag, and at camp, girls raise and lower the flag. Therefore, girls need to learn flag protocol. Here, an older Scout shows a Brownie the proper way to fold the flag.

Girl Scouts visit historic Fort McHenry, where Francis Scott Key composed "The Star-Spangled Banner" on the back of an envelope. Girls learned the history of the fort and the origin of the flag's stars and stripes. They also visited the museum and learned how the fort helped protect Baltimore during the War of 1812.

Brownie and Junior Girl Scouts display unique crafts they created at a troop meeting in the 1990s. Sometimes crafts are made to satisfy badge or patch requirements. Other times they are for a service project. Hospital and nursing home residents really appreciate when the girls come to visit. Often, they would do crafts with the residents

Jousting was designated as Maryland's state sport in 1992. These Girl Scouts are enjoying riding their cardboard steeds while jousting at an outdoor day of fun.

Pictured in the 1990s, these Brownies are earning Science Try-Its (triangular-shaped badges), a fun introduction to the concept of scientific testing. Here, some girls mixed by hand, and others used a fork. It is clear which method scored highest in the fun category.

This very focused Girl Scout carefully transports contents from her archaeological dig. Girl Scouts like outdoor activities which involve having fun and getting dirty.

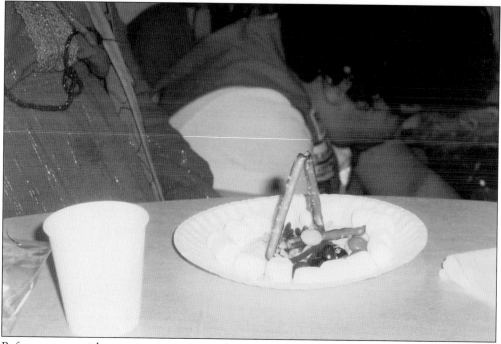

Before younger girls go on a camping trip, they need to learn how to build a campfire. By using the model parts shown here—pretzels and marshmallows—these girls not only learned the proper placement of kindling and timber, they were also allowed to eat the model.

Even indoor campfires allow for s'mores. These girls use the fireplace at Truxton Park to make the delicious, gooey, toasted-marshmallow, chocolate, and graham-cracker sandwiches made famous by the Girl Scouts.

Junior Girl Scouts enjoy roller-skating, part of earning the World of Well-Being badge.

The troop shown here decided to learn what it takes to be a clown. Several women at the Charlestown Retirement Community are members of the Happy Face Clowns clowning unit. The new clowns are coached on how to perform shows for various groups in the area.

Many girls and adults earn faith-based awards where they worship. They work with the clergy to satisfy the badge requirements. Girls receive their awards at a special worship service for Girl Scouts and Boy Scouts.

World Thinking Day, February 22, is a day when Girls Scouts around the world reflect on their sister Scouts and learn more about Girl Scouts and Girl Guides in different countries. This troop is having a program that celebrates native attire.

Troops from all over the nation visit the Juliette Gordon Low birthplace in Savannah, Georgia, to tour the childhood home and grave of the GSUSA founder.

Troops often plan and earn funds from the annual Girl Scout cookie sale to take trips. These girls spent two years earning money for their trip to Niagara Falls.

Girl Scouts and Girl Guides operate four World Centers across the globe: Our Chalet in Switzerland, Our Cabana in Mexico, Sangram in India, and Pax Lodge in England. Senior Girl Scout Maestro Wier, left, and the troop photographed below were able to save enough money to visit Adelboden, Switzerland. Troop and council trips provide Girl Scouts important new experiences; girls may journey individually or as a troop.

The temperatures and elements of the winter did not keep this troop, shown here taking to the slopes, from enjoying the outdoors.

These girls learn to explore marine life in shallow waters using the seining technique, in which a large, shared net is used to gather treasures to study.

Instead of using terrestrial rocks, these girls found that scaling this aquatic rock presented a different climbing challenge. Also, falling was fun.

These Girl Scouts learn basic karate skills and other self-defense techniques, combining learning with fun.

The Brownies photographed here learn how to navigate through the woods using a compass. In recent years, geocaching and letter boxing have become very popular.

Older Girl Scouts may take advantage of high-adventure activities, such as zip-lining, which was part of a ropes course designed to build self-esteem and encourage teamwork.

Girl Scout troops participate in many activities that introduce them to future career possibilities. This Girl Scout is learning about the aerospace field. Many female astronauts were members of Girl Scout troops across the nation and went on to become influential in their chosen careers.

These girls earned a badge while learning how to make and bake Papa John's pizzas.

Photographed at a fabric store, these Girl Scouts are earning a badge by learning to make a quilt. Troop leader Pat Disharoon helped them purchase the necessary materials. When the quilt was finished, the merchant displayed the quilt in her store.

One of the more recent badges Girl Scouts can earn is related to automotive maintenance. In addition to learning basic road and driving safety, girls could learn how to change a tire and the oil as well as other basic forms of maintenance.

Junior Girl Scouts take a tour of WBAL-TV to learn how television news is developed and broadcast to thousands of homes in the Baltimore area. This experience helped girls become aware of the career opportunities (both traditional and nontraditional) that are available in the broadcasting industry.

When the Girl Scouts visited the television station, they tested their meteorology skills. Standing before a green screen, this girl practiced delivering the Baltimore weather, following her hand movements by watching the studio monitor.

Candles are used during the Girl Scout Investiture Ceremony. As shown here, the three large candles symbolize the three parts of the Girl Scout Promise, and the 10 smaller candles represent the 10 parts of the Girl Scout Law.

An enduring tradition among Girl Scouts is the Bridging Ceremony, which is held each year to mark members' progress. Shown here, Juniors bridge to Cadettes.

These photographs were taken on a ship in Baltimore Harbor. Girls and their families gathered onboard for a Bridging Ceremony. They were able to spend the night aboard the ship, and the following morning, they shared breakfast.

In the 1940s, the Curved Bar Award replaced the First Class as the Girl Scouts highest award. Here, two girls receive the Curved Bar at an awards ceremony. During this time, the First Class Award had to be earned before a Girl Scout could receive the Curved Bar.

The Girl Scout photographed here graciously displays her Gold Award portfolio. Gold Award projects address a sustainable community program or service.

A Girls Scout's family members proudly pin the Gold Award on her sash. This reflects the completion of the hard work associated with the Gold Award Community Service Projects.

Having family members pin the Gold Award on the recipient's sash or vest is the highlight of the Gold Award banquet.

When the annual cookie sale approaches, troops plan events so the public knows where and when to buy them. Girl Scouts and cookies became synonymous starting in 1917 in Oklahoma. Until the 1930s, Girl Scouts baked all of the cookies, with mothers providing technical advice. Even then, proceeds supported Girl Scouting at the community level.

Selling techniques have evolved over the years, but creativity and enthusiasm have always been key. As shown here, a well-designed cookie costume and poster, a busy street, and a cheerful marketing team produce winners.

Officials at Fort Meade, Maryland, recognized these girls for their cookie donations to the military. Many Girl Scouts participate in Operation US Mint, a program that is part of the council's Gift of Caring Project. The Operation US Mint initiative provides Girl Scout cookies to the thousands of men and women serving overseas.

This Girl Scout follows founder Juliette Gordon Low's example, "A Girl Scout leaves a place better than she found it."

Four

SWIMMING, S'MORES, AND SONGS

From the earliest days of Juliette Gordon Low's Scouting organization, camping has been an important and popular part of the Girl Scout experience. Camp Mary March opened in 1920 and was the area's first camp site. It served Girl Scouts in Baltimore and Washington, DC. In 1922, Camp Bradley, in Aberdeen, was completed and used as a summer camp for Central Maryland Girl Scouts. In 1927, it was replaced by Camp Whippoorwill, located on the Magothy River, in Anne Arundel County; it is GSCM's oldest camp still in use. In 1935, the Anne Arundel County Girl Scout council was given use of Camp Aberdeen, located along the Aberdeen River in Annapolis, and for nine years, GSCM held summer camp on the site.

In 1944, Camp Woodlands, located on Broad Creek by the South River, was acquired and soon became a favorite venue for summer camping. In 1953 and 1954, the Anne Arundel council built a lodge to accommodate its growing membership. Architect Charles Lamb, whose mother was a council volunteer, designed the structure in the form of a 12-sided polygon, a teepee, with a central fireplace. The structure received an Award of Merit from the American Institute of Architects in 1954.

Camp Ilchester, located in Ellicott City, was purchased in 1949 and is used for day and overnight camping. Today, the campground include indoor program areas and the Caitlin Dunbar Nature Center, a living menagerie comprising native turtles, a flying squirrel, a giant cockroach, a tarantula, and a working beehive. In 1952, the council purchased Deer Creek Camp in northern Baltimore County, which was sold 10 years later because of recurrent floods. In 1953, a 24-acre plot in White Marsh was purchased to facilitate a day camp and Scouts Own ceremonies. It was used until 1975.

Camp Conowingo, the council's largest camp facility—600 acres adjacent to the Susquehanna River in Cecil County—was acquired between 1955 and 1973 and features a 19th-century Victorian mansion (Bell Manor). The camp also comprises Chimney Trail, Shadowbrook, and is the GSCM's summer resident camp program headquarters.

Through camp adventures, girls build new skills and develop an appreciation for nature while making new friends and sharing new experiences. Whether they stay a day, a week or longer, Girl Scout camping activities give girls the opportunity to grow, explore, and have fun—always under the guidance of caring, trained adults. The experiences girls have and the friendships they make create memories that stay with them throughout their lives.

Dear Mom, and dad,
    Thank you for letting me come to camp conowjngo. It was fun I made a good friends Abby and mercy. I have a suprise por you!

        Love,
            Kaity

This letter from Kaity to her parents expresses with sweet simplicity the joys of Girl Scouting. Kaity's letter reflects what Girl Scout Junior Mary expressed when asked what she likes about Scouting: "Amazing camping trips, being with friends, and helping others!" While many troop activities are rewarding and provide girls with similar experiences, camping brings them all together in a unique way that connects to a girl's heart and stays with her.

Although girls today may not think of these outfits as camping attire, until the 1950s, the use of camp uniforms was common. These girls at Camp Bradley are a reminder that taking photographs with friends in front of their tent is a long-standing tradition.

This troop is enjoying some time around the campfire at Camp Bradley around 1920. Their hats reflect the unique nature of some camping attire.

Girls have brought their supplies and are hiking to a primitive campsite. They pack and carry all supplies they will need. Primitive camping is still popular with girls today; good traditions prevail across time.

It was an unpopular and unpleasant Girl Scout rite of passage: cleaning the latrines. Latrine duty was one of several kaper tasks campers shared each day. Other tasks included cooking, making the campfire, and assisting with the flag ceremonies.

Girl Scouts often employ the buddy system. A safety technique, the buddy system helps leaders keep track of a large group, especially when swimming or hiking. When leaders announce a buddy check, pairs find one another and raise their connected hands.

Pictured is the entrance sign to Camp Whippoorwill, which is the Girl Scout camp on the Magothy River.

Totem poles, such as the one pictured below, or other signs were made by camp attendees to identify individual sites within a campground. Robin Hood, Indian Head, Holly Hill, Peter Pan Pines, and Sunset for Peace were some of the area names.

In the 1930s, Girl Scouts at Camp Whippoorwill learned archery, a sport that remains popular today. As with all Girl Scout activities, safety measures are prioritized.

Campers at Camp Whippoorwill rolled up their tent flaps to bring in the breeze. The tents could be adjusted for all weather conditions.

Girl Scouts have always enjoyed water activities, such as sailing and canoeing. Resident campers receive boating, canoeing, and kayaking instructions as well as the rules of safety for all three. Below, the campers prepare to launch canoes.

Campers pictured above and below demonstrate their mastery of the canoeing and kayaking techniques they learned.

Girls at camp cook their supper over an open campfire. In later years, girls also learned indoor cooking techniques. Baltimore chef Nancy Longo attributes her culinary interest to her tenure in the Girl Scouts. Longo prepared meals in Bell Manor kitchen at Camp Conowingo.

These campers use a primitive wash station they learned to set up. The water is in a can, and the paper towels and soap are hung by rope at a level that is beyond the reach of small animals.

Camp Ilchester's Caitlin Dunbar Nature Center is home to critters most girls find challenging: snakes, bees, a giant cockroach, and even a tarantula. The girls below leave handling duties to Ranger "Box Turtle" Heinbuch, shown here with a resident snake.

These girls prove that being up close and learning about worms, crayfish, and other animals can be fun and educational. Shorelines and wooded areas at all four GSCM camps provide a great opportunity to explore wildlife. The Girl Scout shown below definitely likes crayfish.

Camp Conowingo is the only GSCM camp with a pool. Annually, girls have a splashing good time there! Other GSCM camps also have access to water sports through rivers and streams at their camps.

Horsemanship has long been a part of Girl Scout camping, starting from the early days at Camp Bradley. Girls learn about horse care, grooming, mounting, riding, and trotting at the horse corral at Camp Conowingo.

In 1998, GSCM began putting in yurts as tents needed to be replaced. A yurt is a domed, lattice-and-rafter structure that looks like a cross between a cabin and a teepee. Some describe it as a colossal cupcake. Yurts have been in use since at least the 18th century. These 2011 campers easily made this yurt their temporary home.

These girls are taking photographs of their new camp buddies. Many of these special friendships last a lifetime.

Each camp and council has various traditions that have developed over time. At Camp Conowingo, the counselors take round pieces of a tree and sign them. The wood from each year is placed on the fireplace mantel in the dining hall, leaving their legacy for future campers and counselors for years to come.

It is dinnertime, and the girls serve and dine family style. The kaper chart designates a specific chore to each girl, including who will deliver food to the tables.

As in the early days of camping, Girl Scouts still cook over a fire. However, camps now have a kitchen staff that prepares the majority of the meals.

Baltimore's WMAR-TV news reporter Sherrie Johnson visited Camp Conowingo and interviewed director Gail Edwards about the details of camp life and how the experience shapes girls' lives.

In 2011, the United Kingdom's Cheltenham West Rangers visited America to celebrate the centennial year of Girl Guides. They visited Camp Whippoorwill for a week and completed a service project to help set up an astronomy program for Girl Scouts. They donated tools to aid celestial navigation, including a portable planetarium, the National Geographic *Start Navigation* DVD, binoculars, and telescopes. The British girls attended their first baseball game at Oriole Park at Camden Yards.

Five

SERVING COMMUNITIES NEAR AND FAR

The core value of Girl Scouting is service: service to God, service to country, service to people, and service to the world. In her notes on the Girl Scout Law in 1912, Juliette Gordon Low wrote that a girl is to be "loyal and true to her country, to the city or village where she is a citizen, to her family, her church, her school, and those for whom she may work or who may work for her." A Girl Scout is to be helpful at all times, "a giver and not a taker."

Girl Scouts today still promise to serve; they promise to serve their country and the communities in which they live, upholding the principles of the Girl Scout Promise and Law. They also promise to help people at all times, not just girls in their own troop, but to help all in need. By their promise to "protect and improve the world around us," they recognize the great need to serve humanity.

Low set the example of service by her own life. She said, "My purpose is to go on with my heart and soul, devoting all my energy to the Girl Scouts." Over the years, Girl Scouts have participated in local, regional, and national service projects. During World War II, they collected newspapers, became messengers in Baltimore City, and helped farmers in harvesting their crops while the men were away at war.

Today, Central Maryland Girl Scouts carry on the service tradition in their work with organizations that include the Ray Lewis Foundation, Operation Welcome Home, and Maryland Relay for Life. Locally, they are also active in the effort to help restore the Chesapeake Bay.

The Red Feather campaign began during World War II, when several groups merged fundraising efforts and formed the United War Chest. The Red Feather was an icon used on many items of the period to promote the worthy cause.

A local troop chose a butterfly-tagging project that involved catching butterflies, tagging each, and then recording the information. The information could then be accessed by other troops and organizations in the area.

Girls Scouts have a long tradition of bringing cheer to the elderly. This photograph from the 1950s shows a Girl Scout bringing gifts to seniors during the holidays.

Pictured around the 1950s, a Baltimore County forester explains the proper technique for planting and supporting seedling trees, as part of an Arbor Day program. Many troops today still participate in Arbor Day events.

A Daisy Girl Scout brightens the day of a member of the local senior center. This Daisy troop grew the flowers and decorated the flowerpots as gifts to the senior center

Learning about and taking care of the environment is a focus throughout all age levels of Girl Scouting. This Daisy troop demonstrates that commitment as they beautify the grounds of their troop meeting place by planting flowers in the garden.

Save the Bay efforts are extremely popular among Central Maryland Girl Scouts. This troop began a two-year service project to help stabilize the health of a Chesapeake Bay tributary. The girls planted oyster spats (baby oysters) in cages at a pier in Glebe Creek. They monitored their growth and progress until the oysters were large enough to be placed in a sanctuary.

A local Girl Scout troop works to replace the screens and windows on the cabins at Camp Whippoorwill.

These Girl Scouts are showing support for Locks of Love, a nonprofit organization that provides hairpieces to financially disadvantaged children in the United States and Canada experiencing medically related hair loss.

Girl Scouts served as volunteers helping families select and box food during the Ray Lewis Thanksgiving food giveaway for Baltimore City residents.

This troop collected goods for a local food bank and won first prize for the largest donation.

GSCM donated 3,000 pounds of cookies to the Maryland Food Bank to kick off the Harvest for the Hungry food collection campaign. In 2010, a group of 1,603 Girl Scouts collected 77, 909 pounds of food.

Brownie Troop 2011 used its cookie sale proceeds to purchase recycling bins and materials for the first recycling program at their local school. The Brownies held an assembly to explain the program to their schoolmates.

Girls Scouts partnered with the USO to set up "welcome home" booths in the USO lounge. The girls shown here offer prepackaged essentials and Girls Scouts cookies.

Girl Scouts at BWI/Marshall Airport greet military personnel returning home from overseas tours of duty. Girls have the opportunity to talk with soldiers about the hardships of family separations and overseas duties. Most importantly, girls have the opportunity to thank them for their service.

For *Girl Scout Jr. Troop 2609 & Brownie Troop 1032*, the young ladies responsible for smiles across the miles:

We want to thank you for being part of an organization dedicated to teamwork, self-improvement, and to the overall improvement of the world around us—you are the future leaders of America and we're proud of you! We also thank you for thinking of us. The cookies created countless smiles and brought the warmth of American hearts to East Paktika Province, Afghanistan during the Holiday Season.

At Your Service and Very Respectfully,

The Soldiers and Cookie Monsters of Echo Troop, 5th United States Cavalry, Paktika Province, Afghanistan

Junior Troop 2009 and Brownie Troop 1032 received this thank-you note from members of the US Cavalry (and "Cookie Monsters") serving in Afghanistan.

Girl Scouts are always happy to participate in local parades. These girls show their support for the organization that has provided them with so many positive opportunities.

Six

NEW JOURNEYS

Expanding the vision of Juliette Gordon Low among girls and young women has always been the goal of Girl Scout leaders. To that end, the leadership began looking at ways to stay relevant and appealing to girls in the 21st century. The result was a program model that has six clear pathways for participation—troop, events, camp, travel, series, and virtual. The model also includes 15 national leadership outcomes that are associated with the Girl Scout Leadership Experience (GSLE). The Girl Scout Leadership Experience engages girls in discovering self, connecting with others, and taking action to make the world a better place. To enhance the GSLE, Journey books were introduced to the movement. Journey books are age-level activity books that help girls frame topical issues that are all around them, with Girl Scout values. They include profiles of women who used their talents, skills, and abilities to raise public awareness about an issue. The books also include discussions of personal rights, conservation, and advocacy. Journey Awards were also introduced and denote the understanding of leadership concepts presented in the books.

While keeping pace with changing times, there are still traditional aspects of Girl Scouting that remain unchanged. The stalwart tradition of badges remain important hallmarks of skills achieved. Journey Awards recognize growth in three stages of leadership: Discover, Connect, and Take Action. Service, the cornerstone of Girl Scouting operations, continues and is an essential component of earning two of the organization's highest awards, the Silver and Gold Awards. Camping, friendship, and cookies are constants that uniquely distinguish Girl Scout membership and help provide a lifetime of memories. Perhaps Sen. Barbara Mikulski summed it up best when she spoke at an event honoring her support of the organization: "I loved being a Girl Scout . . . we were taught that we could do anything and be anything. We learned values and attitudes that serve as good guides throughout life. We learned how to use a compass, and that gave us a compass for life."

GSCM board chair Sheela Murthy (left) congratulates GSCM chief executive officer Traci Barnett, who was named Innovator of the Year for 2011 by the *Daily Record*. The award is given to Maryland individuals and companies that have created a product, service, program, or process that has had a positive effect on their business. Barnett's award is directly related to the creation of the Science, Technology, Engineering, and Math (STEM) Center at GSCM headquarters in Baltimore.

Ted Imes, director of corporate citizenship at Northrop Grumman, speaks at the 2010 grand opening of the GSCM Urban Program and STEM Center. Imes is flanked on the left by chief executive officer Traci Barnett and on the right by board chair Sheela Murthy. In October 2010, GSCM opened the Urban Program and STEM Center with funding from a Maryland bond bill and generous support from Northrop Grumman.

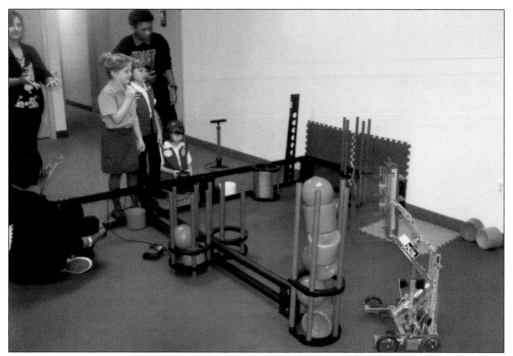

GSCM was able to create the STEM Center, complete with equipment and materials for science, technology, engineering, and math programs; a learning kitchen; a dance studio, and a multimedia room for its Girl Scout members. Older girls, who have been trained using the robotics equipment, are showing a Daisy and Brownies how to use the remote to control a robot.

This is the first Girl Scout program center in Baltimore City and the second Girl Scout Council–owned STEM Center in the nation. GSCM worked with Northrop Grumman, Lockheed Martin, and Johns Hopkins University to assist in providing engaging STEM programs for girls of all ages. These girls are doing an experiment focused on extracting DNA from strawberries.

On October 17, 2011, GSCM honored Sen. Barbara Mikulski, a lifetime Girl Scout, for her longtime support of Girl Scouting and for ensuring that programs like Beyond Bars received federal funding. The entire program center was open with programs for girls of all ages. These girls are in the dance studio practicing a routine to welcome the senator to the event.

The GSCM choir and cheerleaders welcomed guests and speakers as they arrived. A GSCM Beyond Bars troop member shared her experiences with the audience and gave Senator Mikulski special thanks for her support of the program.

In 2011, GSUSA national board chair Connie Lindsey and Sen. Barbara Mikulski spoke at the special event marking the one-year anniversary of the opening of GSCM's STEM Center. They gave inspirational speeches about what Girl Scouting means to them and how being a Girl Scout shaped their lives.

At the event, Sen. Barbara Mikulski was presented with special gifts from the girls of GSCM, including a huge thank-you card from the Beyond Bars troop and a large plaque.

Local police officers work with PAVE campers to provide antiviolence and prevention information during the one-week summer PAVE camp for youth. They also reinforce that police officers are friends that can help in times of trouble.

These PAVE counselors developed a skit, the "Daily Drama," depicting some of the issues teens deal with and the resources teens have to handle these challenges.

Girls at the 2011 PAVE summer camp utilize the STEM Center and learning kitchen for fun and food-related scientific activities. These girls are using marshmallows and spaghetti to build structures as part of an engineering exploration activity.

In the learning kitchen, this young woman is baking miniature pizzas. The kitchen is used to provide educational programs, like Science in the Kitchen, and to help girls learn how to make healthy meals.

The PAVE summer day camp focuses on building self-esteem and character by giving girls an opportunity to talk about friends and the challenges they encounter in and away from school.

These PAVE participants are having a good time acting out a skit and song that expresses some of what they learned over the week.

Pictured is the GSCM headquarters at 4806 Seton Drive in Baltimore City. The building space was expanded in 2010.

This mixed-media mural was created by a group of young women from the Thomas J.S. Waxter Children's Detention Center—who are also Girl Scouts. This troop was formed by volunteer Linda Nape because she believes that every girl can benefit from Girl Scouting. The mural effort was lead by artist David Cunningham, and funds from the Maryland Arts Council, GSCM, and the Arts Council of Anne Arundel County supported the project. The mural celebrates education and achievement for all citizens of Maryland and the talents of every girl, everywhere.

Juliette's Closet is the shop for all things Girl Scouts in Central Maryland. The store has two locations: the council headquarters on Seton Drive and Camp Ilchester in Ellicott City.

The New Girl Scout Leadership Experience (GSLE) introduced innovative ways to participate in the Girl Scout movement. Pathways are the methods in which girls and adults participate in Girl Scouting—like camping, travel, and special events—that are designed to build leadership. Pathways have defined activities and outcomes and offer flexible ways of participation. Journeys are the new books associated with the GSLE. Each Journey provides a sequence of activities, discussions, and challenging experiences that add up to one giant adventure. There are many awards along the way.

This year a new program is being launched called "Journey's". Each Girl Scout starts the journey as a Daisy and follows the various trails until finishing Ambassador.

As the Girl Scouts of Central Maryland, and the nation, continue to explore new worlds, they are reminded of the gift that Juliette Gordon Low gave to so many women when she began Girl Scouting in the United States. Girls today will continue to learn from ongoing traditions, as well as new activities, with an understanding of how far Girl Scouts have come as a community and as an organization. As the women of today teach, help, and encourage the women of tomorrow, today's girls are like the girls riding these horses along the path; for them the path is solid and sure, and the journey is full of wonderful surprises, memories, and life lessons.

MORE ABOUT GSCM

GIRL GUIDE'S PROMISE (1912)
On My Honor, I promise that I will do my best
To do my duty to God and my country.
To help other people at all times.
To obey the Girl Guide Law.

THE GUIDE LAW (1912)
First: A Guide's Honor is to be Trusted.
Second: A Guide is Loyal.
Third: A Guide's Duty is to be Useful and to Help Others.
Fourth: A Guide is a Friend to all, and a Sister to Every Other Guide.
Fifth: A Guide is Courteous.
Sixth: A Guide is a Friend to Animals.
Seventh: A Guide Obeys Orders.
Eighth: A Guide Smiles and Sings.
Ninth: A Guide is Always Pure.
Tenth: A Guide is Thrifty.

GIRL SCOUT PROMISE (LAST REVISED 1984)
On my honor, I will try:
To serve God and my country,
To help people at all times,
And to live by the Girl Scout Law.

THE GIRL SCOUT LAW (LAST REVISED 1996)
I will do my best to be
Honest and fair,
Friendly and helpful,
Considerate and caring,
Courageous and strong, and
Responsible for what I say and do,
And to,
Respect myself and others,
Respect authority,
Use resources wisely,
Make the world a better place,
And be a sister to every Girl Scout.

ANNAPOLIS GIRL SCOUT COUNCIL EXECUTIVE DIRECTOR

1947–1962 Kathleen Lutz

BALTIMORE AREA/GIRL SCOUTS OF CENTRAL MARYLAND EXECUTIVE DIRECTORS AND CEOs

1922	Marguerite Klein
1922	Bertha Howell
1925	Sadie Keating
1927	Mrs. Herbert F. Traut
1928	Carmen McKever
1930	Carolyn Lyder
1954	Hermina G. Stein
1956	Philena Chase Strapelli
1956	June Baetzel
1979	Barbara Minnis
1979	Tina Childs
1983	Beverly Gay Hart
1990	Sherry Welch
1992	Barbara Minnis
1993	Lisa Cid
2002	Traci Barnett

COMMISSIONERS AND PRESIDENTS OF ANNAPOLIS COUNCIL

1945	Ruby Lamb
1950	Mrs. C.P. Brady
1951	Mrs. J.E. Stevens
1953	James G. Stevens
1957	Mrs. Leroy Stevens
1960	Mrs. Sheets
1961	Gail Bunting

BALTIMORE AREA/GIRL SCOUTS OF CENTRAL MARYLAND COMMISSIONERS AND PRESIDENTS

1916	Mrs. Bolling Barton
1922	Emma Warner
1924	Helen H. Carey
1925	Mrs. Walter Hughson
1929	Sophie McLane Fisher
1934	Mary Parlett
1936	Mrs. George Buck
1937	Florence Brennan
1940	Marjorie Paterson
1943	Helen Post Hartz
1948	Eleanor Evens
1951	Selina Wonderlik
1954	Jean Menton
1955	Alberta Schuckle
1957	Clementine Peterson
1959	Margaret Waldschmidt
1962	Mrs. C. Lease Bussard
1963	Ruth Gore
1968	Jean Culwell
1971	Irma Marquart
1975	Mary Ruth Dowling
1978	Betty Hall
1982	Dr. Thelma Banks Cox
1986	Patsy Davis
1990	Marilyn Maultsby
1992	Patsy Davis
1996	Sandra McNeill
2000	Rosalind McElrath
2002	Mary McClurg
2006	Dawn S. Hyde
2007	Donna Reihl
2010	Sheela Murthy, Esq.

ANNAPOLIS COUNCIL OFFICES

1950 Scout Office in Capital Gazette Building
1962 Scout Office in Speer Building, 3 Church Circle

COUNCIL OFFICES THROUGH THE YEARS (ALL LOCATED IN BALTIMORE)

1917	Children's Association Building, 7 West Mulberry Street
1922	13 West Franklin Street
1925	525 North Charles Street
1929	1931 St. Paul Street, at the corner of Read Street
1940	827 St. Paul Street
1945	10 West Chase Street
1953	128 West Franklin Street (YMCA)
1968	2518 Greenmount Avenue
1976	1976 Singley Building, Keswick Home
1996	4806 Seton Drive

DISCOVER THOUSANDS OF LOCAL HISTORY BOOKS FEATURING MILLIONS OF VINTAGE IMAGES

Arcadia Publishing, the leading local history publisher in the United States, is committed to making history accessible and meaningful through publishing books that celebrate and preserve the heritage of America's people and places.

Find more books like this at
www.arcadiapublishing.com

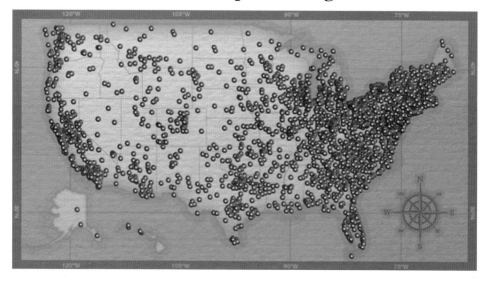

Search for your hometown history, your old stomping grounds, and even your favorite sports team.

Consistent with our mission to preserve history on a local level, this book was printed in South Carolina on American-made paper and manufactured entirely in the United States. Products carrying the accredited Forest Stewardship Council (FSC) label are printed on 100 percent FSC-certified paper.

MADE IN THE USA